# MAORI

Leslie Strudwick

**WEIGL PUBLISHERS INC.**

Published by Weigl Publishers Inc.
350 5ᵗʰ Avenue, Suite 3304, PMB 6G
New York, NY  10118-0069  USA
Web site: www.weigl.com

All of the Internet URLs given in the book were valid at the time of publication.
However, due to the dynamic nature of the Internet, some addresses may have changed,
or sites may have ceased to exist since publication. While the author and publisher regret any
inconvenience this may cause readers, no responsibility for any such changes can be accepted
by either the author or the publisher.

Library of Congress Cataloging-in-Publication Data

Strudwick, Leslie, 1970-
  Maori / Leslie Strudwick.
     p. cm. -- (Indigenous peoples)
  Includes index.
  ISBN 1-59036-221-7 (lib. bdg. : alk. paper) 1-59036-256-X (softcover)
  1.  Maori (New Zealand people)--Juvenile literature.  I. Title. II. Series.
  DU423.A1S77 2005
  305.89'9442--dc22

                              2004005773


Printed in the United States of America
1 2 3 4 5 6 7 8 9 0   08 07 06 05 04

**Project Coordinator** Heather C. Hudak  **Design** Terry Paulhus  **Layout** Katherine Phillips
and Jeff Brown  **Copy Editor** Janice L. Redlin  **Photo Research** Wendy Cosh and Ellen Bryan


**Consultant** James Heremaia

# CONTENTS

**Where in the World?** .................. **4**

**Stories and Legends** .................. **6**

**Out of the Past** ...................... **8**

**Social Structures** .................... **10**

**Communication** ...................... **12**

**Law and Order** ...................... **14**

**Celebrating Culture** .................. **16**

**Art and Culture** ...................... **18**

**Dressing Up** ........................ **20**

**Food and Fun** ....................... **22**

**Great Ideas** ......................... **24**

**At Issue** ............................ **26**

**Into the Future** ...................... **28**

**Fascinating Facts** .................... **30**

**Glossary** ........................... **31**

**Index and Photograph Credits** ........ **32**

# Where in the World?

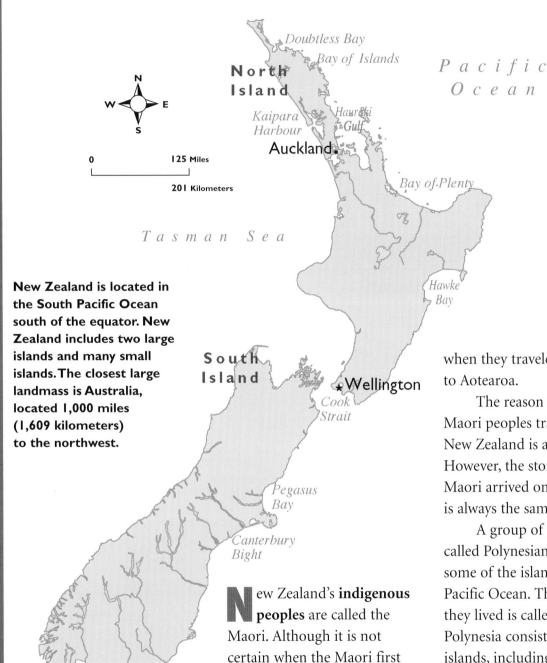

*Doubtless Bay*

*Bay of Islands*

**North Island**

*P a c i f i c O c e a n*

*Kaipara Harbour*

*Hauraki Gulf*

**Auckland.**

*Bay of Plenty*

*T a s m a n   S e a*

**New Zealand is located in the South Pacific Ocean south of the equator. New Zealand includes two large islands and many small islands. The closest large landmass is Australia, located 1,000 miles (1,609 kilometers) to the northwest.**

*Hawke Bay*

**South Island**

**★Wellington**

*Cook Strait*

*Pegasus Bay*

*Canterbury Bight*

*Foveaux Strait*

**Stewart Island**

N
W E
S

0 — 125 Miles

201 Kilometers

New Zealand's **indigenous peoples** are called the Maori. Although it is not certain when the Maori first began arriving on New Zealand, or **Aotearoa**, most archaeologists believe it was between AD 950 and AD 1130. Even Maori oral history and legends suggest this is the time in history when they traveled to Aotearoa.

The reason why the Maori peoples traveled to New Zealand is also a mystery. However, the story of how the Maori arrived on this new land is always the same.

A group of people called Polynesians lived on some of the islands in the Pacific Ocean. The area where they lived is called Polynesia. Polynesia consists of many islands, including Tahiti, the Cook Islands, Hawai'i, and Easter Island off the coast of South America. The Polynesians were the first group of people to set sail for the distant, unsettled land of Aotearoa. They traveled in

The Maori name for New Zealand's South Island is *Te Wai Pounamu*, which means "the Greenstone Water."

huge canoes that carried more than 100 people each. This group of Polynesian voyagers is known as the Great Fleet. While stories tell of several hundred people who arrived on Aotearoa at the same time, some researchers today believe there were much fewer people in the group.

When the Maori arrived at Aotearoa, they found a very different land than the tropical islands from which they came. The temperature was cooler, there were different plants and trees, and there were no land mammals, just reptiles, birds, and sea life. Most early Maori settled on the northern island of Aotearoa because it was warmer, but some groups settled on the South Island, as well.

The Maori quickly adapted to life on Aotearoa. They learned to hunt and fish the wildlife in the region. Many of the islands' birds could not fly, including a large ostrich-like bird called the **moa**. Moas were hunted and used as food. The settlers used moa bones to make tools and ornaments. They used moa eggshells to carry water.

The settlers learned to grow crops after they hunted some of the animals, such as the moa, to extinction. Small settlements became large villages once these indigenous peoples settled and began farming.

- Aotearoa's land area is a total of 103,470 square miles (267,990 square kilometers).

- The largest lake in Aotearoa is Lake Taupo. This lake has an area of 234 square miles (606 sq km).

- Aotearoa is home to more than 1,500 plant species that are not found anywhere else in the world. Some of these plants are the kauri, totara, and rimu.

- The only land mammals that live naturally on Aotearoa are bats. Humans brought all other land mammals to the islands.

# Stories and Legends

**Maori legends explained the relationship between people, the land, and the sea.**

Like many other **cultures**, the Maori used legends to explain the origins of their culture and the creation of land, water, and humans.

According to Maori legend, in the beginning of time nothing existed, only darkness. The sea, Earth, and gods had not been created. The Moon, the Sun, and the Heavens were created from the darkness. Soon after, the first Maori people were born from this nothingness. They were the Sky Father, named Ranginui, and the Earth Mother, named Papatuanuku. The Father and the Mother arrived on Earth together. As they traveled to Earth, they embraced. This embrace covered the sunlight, and there was darkness again.

Ranginui and Papatuanuku had 70 male children. These children became the many gods the Maori worship. Ranginui and Papatuanuku remained embraced around their children. The children tired of living in darkness. In order to have light, Ranginui and Papatuanuku's children realized they must separate their parents.

Many of the children struggled to separate Ranginui and Papatuanuku, but it was Tane-Mahuta, the god of forests, who succeeded.

He believed Ranginui should live in the sky and Papatuanuku should live on Earth.

Light shone down on the children after Ranginui and Papatuanuku were separated. However, the Sky Father was heartbroken. His tears created the oceans. Tawairi Matea, who was the god of wind and storms, was angry with his brothers for separating his parents. He created the winds and storms in revenge. Tawairi Matea decided to join his father in the sky.

After the creation of the sky and Earth, Tane realized there was something missing on Earth. He created woman from clay and breathed life into her. This Earth-formed woman was Hine-hauone. She and Tane had a daughter named Hinetitama, who later became the goddess of the night.

## THE STORY OF HOW MAUI DISCOVERED AOTEAROA

One day when Maui, a demi-god, was very young, he hid in his brother's fishing boat. The brothers did not find Maui until they were too far from shore to turn back.

The brothers continued rowing out to sea. Once they were quite far from shore, Maui dropped his magic fishhook into the water. Soon, he felt a strong tug on the line. Maui called to his brothers for help.

After much hard work, the brothers pulled the North Island of Aotearoa from the water. Maui thought the gods might be angry, so he went to make peace.

While Maui was gone, the brothers fought to control the new land. They pounded the island with their weapons. This created mountains and valleys.

According to Maori legend, an ancient navigator named Kupe discovered Aotearoa while in pursuit of a giant octopus.

# Out of the Past

The explorer Able Tasman was attacked by powerful Maori warriors at Massacre Bay when he traveled to New Zealand in 1642.

Traditional Maori families lived together in villages. Each village had several tribes, or *iwi*. Each member of the iwi was related through a common **ancestor**. Each tribe was made up of many sub-tribes, or *hapu*. About 500 people lived in one hapu.

The land on which a hapu lived and farmed was owned by all the people in the tribe. Individuals did not own land. Each village settlement may have had one or many hapu.

Often, the land on which a hapu lived was valuable. This caused fighting between some tribes. Land was symbolic of power, **prestige**, and wealth. Many tribes needed more land as their villages grew. Warfare was an important aspect of

Maori life. However, fighting only occurred during times when the Maori could not grow crops or hunt. The chores involved with these activities were more important than fighting.

Settling into villages changed the Maori's traditional way of life. Another important change took place when

**Captain James Cook sailed to New Zealand on the *Endeavour*. The *HM Bark Endeavour* is an exact working replica of Cook's ship.**

European settlers began arriving on Aotearoa.

In 1642, a Dutch explorer named Abel Tasman was the first European to visit the region. It was not until more than 100 years later, when Captain James Cook arrived, that the Maori felt the impact of European settlers.

The Maori called European settlers *Pakeha*. At first, the Maori welcomed the Pakeha to their land. The Europeans brought new tools and materials to the Maori. They taught the Maori new farming methods. However, the Europeans also brought diseases to the Maori. Many became ill and died after contracting these diseases.

The Europeans brought weapons and alcohol to Aotearoa. Traditionally, battles between Maori tribes were fought with spears, knives, and clubs. With the Pakehas' muskets, the Maori killed each other in record numbers during wars.

The first Christian **missionaries** arrived in New Zealand in 1814. Christian missionaries were also called Pakehas. While the Maori did not want to learn about Christianity, the missionaries taught them how to read and write. The Maori's way of life was quickly disappearing.

**A.D. 950–1130** Polynesian settlers arrive on Aotearoa

**1642** Dutch explorer Abel Tasman is the first European explorer to encounter the Maori. The Maori kill four of Tasman's crew members

**1769** Captain James Cook meets the Maori

**1800s** European settlers begin to arrive on Aotearoa

**1840** The Maori and the British government sign the Treaty of Waitangi, granting Britain rule of the island and promising the Maori British citizenship and rights

**1841** Aotearoa becomes a British colony

**1860–1872** The New Zealand Wars begin over land claims

**1920s** Maori art and culture is thriving

**1980s** More than 90 percent of the Maori population lives in cities

**1995** Queen Elizabeth of Great Britain issues a formal apology to the Maori for their loss of lives and property in the 1800s

# Social Structures

**Maniaro Marae is located on a hill overlooking the sea near the town of Moku. It is an important place for the Maori community to gather for meetings, rituals, and other cultural events.**

Each traditional Maori village followed a specific structure. Villages were fortified to protect them from attack by other Maori tribes. These villages were called *pa*. Within the village, there was a main meeting house called a *whare*. If the village was large, there may be more than one whare. A whare was usually located in the center of a village. The Maori built a large, public meeting area, called a *marae*, in front of the whare.

Whares were **sacred** buildings where the Maori believed they were in the presence of their ancestors. These buildings were decorated with intricate carvings and weaving. Some sub-tribes also built whares, where they could gather with their own family and call upon their ancestors.

Each tribe had a chief, or *rangatira*. The chief had a **privileged** life. He lived, dressed, and ate very well. Some chiefs had more than one wife. Chiefs could also have **slaves**. These slaves were usually people who were captured during wars. Each village had a *tohunga*, who was a healer, wise man, or priest.

Some tribe members belonged to a higher **rank**.

Others belonged to a lower rank. Rank was not based on a person's possessions. Instead, rank was often determined by how much work a person did for the tribe. People who served or provided the most for the village had the highest ranks. Rank was also determined by family status. Being a chief's close relative gave a person a higher standing in the village.

Warfare was a part of Maori life. Preparing for battle was also a social **rite** of passage. Boys were expected to be warriors. At a young age, they learned **martial arts** and how to use weapons. Weapons were made from wood, whalebone, and greenstone, which is a type of very hard stone called jade. Preserving the tribe's honor was often a reason to go to war. Prestige, or *mana*, was extremely important to the Maori. Warriors wanted to protect their own mana and try to damage other tribes' mana.

Maori men performed a dance called the *haka* to prepare for battle. This dance included heavy stomping, loud chanting, and aggressive body movements.

## THE SEASONS

New Zealand's seasons are opposite to the Northern Hemisphere. December through February is summer. These are the warmest months. March through May is autumn. June through August is winter. Spring is September through November. November is the rainiest month.

# Communication

**The Maori style of storytelling is known as *Maoritanga*. Stories pass on Maori culture from one generation to the next.**

Public speaking was an important form of communication for the Maori. Any person who could inspire through speaking was held in high regard. The Maori did not have a written language until missionaries arrived in the 1800s. As a result, the spoken word became very important and valued. Public speaking included giving speeches, reciting poetry, singing songs, chanting, passing on history, or telling a joke or a story. It was a form of expression.

Stories were passed down orally from one **generation** to the next. Gifted storytellers spoke poetically. They would repeat stories and legends in great detail. The storyteller's voice became soft, loud, or angry to make a story more dramatic and to show many emotions. Songs were often sung within the telling of a story. The storyteller would also move about and make arm gestures, jump, or walk to add to the story.

Songs told stories, as well. Songs expressed what was important to the Maori by using words about nature, traditions, or even jokes. Many of the songs the Maori sing today are about mourning or love. Maori women composed many of these love songs.

Before missionaries created a written language, the Maori used a series of carving signs and knots to communicate. European missionaries used the English alphabet to represent the different sounds they heard in the Maori language. Only fifteen letters or letter combinations are used to write the sounds of Maori words. These letters and combinations are h, k, m, n, p, r, t, w, a, e, i, o u, wh, and ng. Each syllable ends with a vowel sound.

The first Maori language dictionary was written in 1844. Bishop Henry W. Williams compiled the information for this dictionary. He believed by learning about the Maori language and culture, he could convert more Maori to Christianity. Once the Maori learned to communicate by reading and writing, they considered these skills quite valuable.

# THE CHANGING LANGUAGE

Originally, the Maori language was a **dialect** of the Polynesian language. Eventually, the Maori language developed its own characteristics.

Over time, the Maori language changed to include words that describe European items or events. For example, the Maori borrowed the word *hoʻiho* from the English word "horse," and the word *taʻone* from the English word *"town."*

The Maori have borrowed words from languages other than English, as well. For example, the Maori word *miʻere* came from the French word *miel*, which means "honey."

**The *hongi* is a traditional Maori greeting. Two people press their noses lightly together to exchange the *ha*, or breath of life.**

# Law and Order

Traditional Maori society did not need laws and government. Instead, the Maori lived their lives according to their sense of honor, or mana, and according to *tapu*. Tapu is similar in meaning to the English language word "taboo," which means something sacred or forbidden. Tapu governed their lives and their beliefs.

Many things in Maori society were considered tapu. These things were governed by the village's tohunga, or spiritual leader. Certain places, such as a marae, were tapu. Some objects were also tapu, as were certain activities and even people. People in a village were ranked, and it was tapu for members of a higher rank to touch objects that belonged

Conch shell trumpets called *putatara* were valuable possessions. They were used for a variety of purposes, including signaling and ceremonial rituals.

to a person of a lower rank. Should a higher ranked person touch one of these objects, it was considered pollution. The reverse was much worse. If a person of a lower rank touched an object belonging to someone of a higher rank, the person of the lower rank could be sentenced to death.

Many items belonging to a chief were tapu. For example, a chief's house was tapu. Women could not enter his house unless a special ceremony was performed.

Food was often tapu, too. Some foods could not be eaten inside a home, especially a chief's home. Food cooked for a chief was tapu and could not be eaten by anyone of a lower rank. Even if the chief did not eat it, it was tapu for a person of a lower rank to eat the food.

It was rare for a member of the Maori community to act against the tapu. While breaking these tapu did not go unpunished, the Maori believed the real punishment would come from the gods. They believed terrible things would happen to someone who acted against a tapu.

Tapu is still a part of modern Maori culture. A new house may have a *noa* ceremony to remove the tapu. This makes the house safe for the new residents.

# Celebrating Culture

Traditional Maori culture was centered around daily life and chores. Hunting, fishing, and growing crops were as much a part of Maori culture as they were a way to survive. Since most members of a Maori village were somehow related, all tribe members were responsible for and to each another.

Mothers and fathers raised their sons and daughters, but grandparents, aunts, uncles, and cousins sometimes watched or taught the children.

Elders used stories to teach children. The Maori have a rich oral history, and stories are passed down from one generation to the next. Public speaking was an important part of Maori culture, and chiefs were especially talented. When a chief or any other tribe member told a story, this person tried to make it dramatic and entertaining to watch.

Dances, or *haka*, were performed as a way of showing happiness or in preparation for war. There were two types of haka before a war. One was performed without weapons. It was used to express the warriors'

Haka are often passed from generation to generation. Modern haka can include political themes such as child abuse and the September 11, 2001 terrorist attacks.

feelings. The other haka was called *peruperu*. It was usually performed before setting off into battle. The warriors would make fierce facial expressions, shout and grunt, stick out their tongue, and wave their weapons. This haka was used to invoke the god of war and warn the enemy of the fate that would soon come to them. These dances were performed in complete unity. A tribal elder inspected the warriors as the haka was performed. It was considered a bad omen if the group did not perform as one.

Although haka are no longer performed to prepare for war, many Maori groups still perform these dances. They do this to stay connected to their culture and their tribe. Tourists also enjoy seeing the lively performances.

The haka is popular in New Zealand. Some sports teams have their own haka that they perform before each game. The New Zealand Army has a haka that each recruit must learn and perform.

# Art and Culture

**A double or single spiral pattern called *pitau* is used on every Maori carving.**

**A**rt was an important part of Maori culture. The Maori decorated the walls, pillars, and ceilings of their homes. They decorated their clothes, weapons, boats, personal objects, and even their bodies, too.

Carving is an important form of Maori artwork. History was passed on through storytelling, but it was also done through carvings.

When the Maori first settled in Aotearoa, their carvings were still similar to that of other Polynesian groups. As they became a unique culture, they created their own carving style from the materials available in their new surroundings.

Inside the traditional homes of Maori chiefs, the wood is carved with very detailed patterns. The Maori sometimes carved their ancestor's faces or their own face into the wood. The Maori also recreated the shapes of fish, whales, animals, or their gods. The Maori took great care when creating these carvings. The wooden handles of spears, knives, and other weapons also included detailed carvings. The stone that was used to make the point of a spear was created with just as much care as the carved handle. Carvings were also done according to tapu, which made them even more meaningful.

Wood, especially from the totara and kauri pine trees, was a popular material to carve. Maori men also made carvings from whale's teeth, stone, bone, and seal ivory. Not every Maori man was a carver. It was a talent only **honed** by some, and these men had a high standing in the village. Master carvers taught children how to carve.

While men would carve, women would weave. Weaving took just as much care to

The art of flax weaving, or *harakeke*, is passed down from generation to generation. Traditionally, women learned how to weave flax at an early age.

create as carving. Women used reeds or products from their crops, such as **flax**, to create their weaves. They made clothing, baskets, footwear, and panels that would cover the walls of their homes.

Women wove beautiful panes with various designs that would **adorn** the walls between carved wooden pillars.

# MAORI PERFORMANCE

Music and dance are important parts of Maori culture. Traditionally, the word haka is used to describe all kinds of performances, including dance. Often, warriors performed the haka before a battle. During this type of haka, warriors chanted loudly while stamping their feet and moving their arms. Each tribe has its own haka.

Festivals featuring these activities take place throughout the year. Many of the best Maori performers compete during these festivals.

# Dressing Up

Maori women included detailed weaving on the clothes they made. Flax was the most common material used to make clothes. Women also made clothes from cabbage-tree leaves, dog skin and fur, feathers, and sometimes even human hair. The garments they created were often stiff and uncomfortable. All the materials were woven together by hand. The women did not have **looms**.

Girls were taught how to weave at a very young age.

**Maori traditional dress is worn for ceremonies and cultural performances. Some clothing is made in the traditional way. Other clothing is made using new techniques and materials.**

It was a skill all girls needed to learn. The tohunga blessed girls who were especially talented at weaving.

Maori men and women wore different styles of clothing, as did people of higher or lower ranks. The Maori also wore different clothing for special occasions. While garments made out of dog skin were at one time the most prized clothing items, those made out of feathers

from the kiwi bird became more prestigious over time. The Maori adorned themselves with pendants, combs, and feathers as a way to decorate their clothing.

Another way the Maori "dressed up" or decorated themselves was by tattooing their skin. Tattooing was considered a way to carve their skin. The Maori cut patterns into their skin using tiny **chisels**. Then, they would tap dye into the cuts. It was a long and painful process; however, tattoos were considered to be full of mana. Most Maori men tattooed their bodies. They made designs on their faces, thighs, and buttocks. The head was considered the most sacred party of the body, so the head was very elaborately tattooed. If a Maori woman tattooed her face, it was usually along the upper lip, around the nostrils, or on the chin.

Tattooing different parts of the face was symbolic of many things. For example, a man's forehand was tattooed with his rank. Tattoos beneath a man's eyes were related to his family tree. Tattooing the part of the face that is directly in front of the ears symbolized if a man was married.

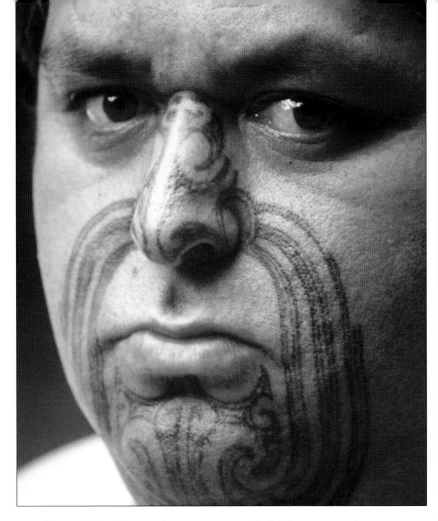

Traditional Maori tattooing was very painful. A person who was being tattooed could not eat solid food. Instead, liquid food was served through a wooden funnel.

## CLOAKS FOR COVER

Maori women practice special weaving methods to create traditional **cloaks**. These cloaks, which are made to honor a family member or a tribe member, take many months of preparing and handweaving to create. Cloaks are often made from flax fiber.

Cloaks are often passed down from one generation to the next. These cloaks are highly valued, and the Maori wear them for special occasions, such as graduation and ceremonies. Today, only a few Maori women are able to make traditional cloaks.

# Food and Fun

**Food cooked in a traditional Maori *hangi* is very tender, with a unique, earthy flavor.**

The Maori brought their most important crop with them from Polynesia. This crop was called *kumara*, and it was similar to a sweet potato. Kumara was a main staple in the Maori diet. At first, the Maori had difficulty growing kumara on Aotearoa, but they found ways to make this crop grow well in their new climate. They also found ways to store the kumara during the colder winter months.

Since all the members of a village hunted and grew food as a group, they also stored, cooked, and ate their food together. Kumara was stored in large, deep, cool pits that were built on hillsides.

## ROROI RECIPE

- Peel and wash six kumara. Grate four, and slice two.
- Butter a baking dish. Place sliced kumara on the bottom of the dish, and sprinkle with water.
- Place grated kumara on top of the slices. Sprinkle brown sugar and butter on top.
- Add another layer of each, finishing with a layer of sliced kumara, butter, and brown sugar.
- Cover with foil and bake at 356 degrees Fahrenheit (180 degrees Celsius) for 45 to 60 minutes.

The Maori hunted many different species of birds for food, including the kereru and the tui.

Proper food storage was very important. In fact, the Maori created storehouses, called *patakas*, for food.

Like all buildings, patakas were decorated with carvings. The carvings were **fertility** symbols, which the Maori hoped would encourage the gods to provide a generous supply of food.

The Maori were skilled hunters and fishers. They wove flax nets to catch fish. They carved fishhooks from bone and stone. The Maori also used spears to hunt birds and fish.

Birds, fish, seals, shellfish, and sometimes whales were other foods that were included in the Maori's diet. The Maori cooked food in an area that was not located near where they lived and slept. It was tapu to live and eat in the same building. Often, they cooked food out in the open air or in a shelter. Many families ate together. They cooked their food in a large pit called a *hangi* or *umu*. The Maori placed stones over a fire of wooden sticks. They placed a layer of green flax on top of the stones. Meat and vegetables were on top of the flax and then covered with another piece of flax. The Maori covered the oven with a mat. Then, they poured water over the stones to steam the food.

Children and adults enjoyed playing games and having fun. They played many games that taught them valuable skills. For example, young boys threw soft spears at each other to practice their battle skills. Boys also enjoyed walking on stilts.

The Maori spent a great deal of time around the water. Young Maori would swing from ropes into a river or water below. They would also body surf in the ocean.

Kites were mostly flown by children, but the village tohunga had his own special version of a kite. String games, puppets, and playing musical instruments, such as a flute made from wood or a trumpet made from shells, were also forms of entertainment.

# Great Ideas

Traditionally, the Maori depended on items they found in nature for their survival. As a result, they respected all aspects of nature. This included trees, water, land, birds, and all animals.

As a form of respect, the Maori named large trees. When they needed to cut down one of these trees, the Maori held a ceremony to honor the tree. The tree was then used to build items such as shelters in the village or weapons for hunting and battles. No matter how the tree was used, it was likely carved and decorated.

Although weapons or ornaments made from greenstone have been found on both the North Island and South Island of Aotearoa, the stone used to create these items came from the South Island. This meant that the Maori traded with or gave generous gifts to other villages. While many Maori tribes warred with each other, others also visited and benefited from each other. When one tribe visited another tribe, the visiting tribe brought gifts of thanks to their hosts. Later, the host tribe was invited to visit the tribe they had hosted. This tribe brought even more generous gifts to the host tribe. Tribes from the South Island may have given gifts of greenstone-tipped spears when they visited northern tribes. A coastal

**Wood was a very important part of Maori culture. Homes, boats, weapons, and spiritual artifacts were made from wood products. Maori carvings are famous for their elaborate detail.**

tribe may have given a generous portion of fish to a village that was inland.

While many Maori tribes had friendly relations, others sometimes fought in wars. The Maori had many war strategies. When the Maori began living in larger villages with more families, they built these villages in places that were safe from attack, such as on hills, along rivers, or by the sea. Much like a fort, great walls surrounded these villages. These villages were called *pa*.

Hand-to-hand combat was not the only way the Maori fought their wars. They prided themselves on tricking their enemy. Sometimes a visiting tribe might attack their host tribe during a feast. Surprising the tribe that was under attack was often key to a victory. However, it was not uncommon for a tribe to feed their hungry opposers to ensure they were fighting on an "even" playing field. An easy victory over weaker opponents was not as honorable. Honor was very important to the Maori.

# WEAPONS FOR WAR

While the Maori fought many battles against British soldiers, sometimes, Maori tribes also battled against each other. Regardless of the situation, the Maori had many special battle weapons.

The Maori carved weapons out of greenstone, wood, and bone. Each warrior had his own weapon, which was carved with a special symbol. The Maori used many weapons for war, but there were three main weapons. These weapons could kill even the strongest warrior with only one hit.

The *taiaha* was a long, pointed staff that looked like a spear. The pointed end was carved in the shape of a face that had paua shell eyes and a long, pointed tongue. The Maori used feathers and dog hair to decorate the shaft just below the face.

*Patu* were short clubs that warriors wore on their flax belts. The Maori used this weapon to strike or beat their enemies.

The *tewhatewha* had a long handle with an axelike blade at one end and a point at the other end.

# At Issue

The Maori worked hard to maintain their culture as Pakeha settlements increased and the Maori population declined. They preserved their culture and traditional skills such as jade carving.

When the Pakeha arrived on Aotearoa, it was not long before the land officially became New Zealand. This newly formed country was part of the British Empire. Although there had been battles between the Maori and the Pakeha, the Maori agreed to live under British rule. In 1840, the Maori and the British government signed the Treaty of Waitangi. This treaty was created to protect the Maori and the land they lived on, as well as provide the Maori with the same rights as the British settlers.

Soon, Maori land was sold to Pakeha settlers, and the Maori were not allowed to live on some of the best land. From 1845 to 1870, more battles took place between the British and the Maori. The Maori were not successful.

By the 1870s, many Maori chiefs and their tribes had died in the land wars. In addition, the British government claimed more than 3 million acres (1,214,057 hectares) of Maori land.

The Maori population was quickly declining. Many Maori were killed in the Maori Wars. Thousands of the Maori died from diseases that settlers brought with them from other countries.

When the British government took control over Aotearoa, money became important for survival. The Maori had not used currency in exchange for goods. This was a new idea for the Maori. Some Maori groups wanted to return to traditional ways and form their own societies. Other Maori tried to live the new life that was being introduced. With no money or means to live, more Maori died. By 1900, there were only about 40,000 Maori left. Many people referred to the Maori as a "dying race."

In order for the Maori to survive, they would need to fight. Due to the declining Maori population, battle was no longer an option. Instead, the Maori lobbied the government, negotiated deals, or hired lawyers to represent them in courtroom battles. Since the 1980s, many historical treaty disputes have been settled. Usually, the Maori receive a formal apology for the way they were treated by the settlers. They also receive money and land.

In 1975, the Waitangi Tribunal was created so Waitangi Treaty claims could be researched. While the tribunal does not settle claims and disputes, it makes recommendations to the government. These recommendations suggest ways the claim may be resolved or if the claim should be addressed. Claims are settled through negotiation with the government.

# MAORI LAND PROTESTS

During the 1970s, the Maori continued to struggle for the land rights they were promised in the Treaty of Waitangi. Land protests became a powerful way to lobby the government. There were many land marches and protests, which helped lead to the creation of the Maori Affairs Amendment Act in 1974, the parliamentary election of two Maori representatives in 1975, and the creation of the Waitangi Tribunal in 1975.

In 1970, one of the largest protest groups, Nga Tamatoa, formed to lobby for Maori cultural identity and acknowledgement of Maori issues.

In 1975, Dame Whina Cooper led the Maori land rights march from the top of the North Island to the Parliament buildings in Wellington. Maori protesters from all over Aotearoa marched alongside Cooper.

In 1978, Eva Rickard led 4 years of non-violent protest to reclaim Tanui land, which was used for defense purposes and later made into a golf course.

On May 5, 2004, thousands of Maori protested outside parliament in Wellington, New Zealand. They wanted to stop the government from nationalizing the New Zealand shoreline that traditionally belonged to the Maori.

# Into the Future

By 1769, there were fewer than 85,000 Maori living on the islands of Aotearoa. They needed to find new ways to survive and to build a strong community. They had done this before, when they first came to Aotearoa, and they would need to do it again.

Beginning in 1867, four Maori representatives could be elected to the New Zealand government. At first, the Maori did not realize the importance of political power. However, by the 1900s, some Maori groups understood the need to have political representation. These groups began forming their own political parties, such as the Young Maori Party.

In 1994, the Queen of England, Elizabeth II, apologized to the Maori for how they were treated when the settlers first arrived and for the great loss the Maori people and their culture suffered.

Some Maori leaders decided to find ways to make Western values work within their traditional values. They saw the importance of education, proper **sanitation**, and building a strong economy. These leaders and other Maori groups realized the need to maintain their traditional society, as well as acquire the benefits of modern technology. Rather than being ashamed of their history, they wanted to rebuild their dying culture. There was renewed

Maori was declared an official language in New Zealand in 1987. In 2001, one in four Maori people spoke the Maori language. Radio and television networks now broadcast in Maori, too.

interest in traditional ways of life. This rebuilding of the Maori culture continues today. While their language had once been banned from schools, it is now being taught to Maori students.

Life for the Maori today is far from perfect. For many, daily living is still a struggle. Many of the Maori are trying to adapt to new technology. Traditional Maori communities were small and family based. All members of the tribe lived and worked together. They worked to supply their tribe with food and clothing. This is how they achieved a higher status in their community.

Today, most Maori live in cities. They must become more independent because they do not have a large tribe

Today, Maori people work in industries such as tourism and entertainment. The final battle scenes of *The Last Samurai* were filmed on farmland near Taranaki in 2003.

to provide for them. Working for money is different from the traditional ways of the Maori. They have had to change many of their ways of life in a short period of time.

The Maori are a group of survivors. With attention placed on the importance of keeping their traditional values, they are mixing the best of the old with the best of the new.

Their population is increasing, too. In 2000, nearly 600,000 Maori were living in New Zealand. This is 15 times greater than just 100 years earlier.

## DAME WHINA COOPER

Born in 1895, Dame Whina Cooper was the daughter of a Maori chief. Cooper led many Maori rights movements in an effort to reclaim Maori land and maintain traditional ways of life.

Cooper's actions resulted in land developments in the North Auckland region, the establishment of the Maori Women's Welfare League, and the creation of the Te Unga Waka Community Centre in Auckland. Cooper also led the land march in 1975. Cooper was made a Dame of the Order of the British Empire in 1980. She was admitted to the Order of New Zealand in 1991. Cooper died in 1994.

# Fascinating Facts

- About 16 percent of New Zealand's population is Maori.

- More than 95 percent of Maori live on the North Island of New Zealand.

- Two people pressing their noses together is a traditional Maori greeting called hongi.

- The Pacific Islands where the Maori first lived was called Hawaiiki.

- While men had their faces tattooed, they ate liquid food poured through a wooden funnel. It was tapu for cooked food to touch the man's lips.

- The Maori introduced land mammals to New Zealand. They brought dogs and rats with them from Hawaiiki.

- Reptiles, birds, bats, and sea mammal are the only animals native to New Zealand.

- The Maori preserved the heads of warriors. At one time, if a chief died in battle, his head was cut off and dried so his tribesmen could take it home for a proper funeral.

- The Maori often fought wars for revenge over mana they had lost. Sometimes a tribe would not war over mana until generations after it was lost.

- Although the Maori had flute- and trumpet-like instruments, they did not have drums. They stamped their feet for rhythm. The closest instrument to a drum was a gong.

## FURTHER READING

Lockyer, John. *A History of New Zealand.* Auckland: Reed Books, 2002.

Reed, A. W. *Maori Myth and Legend.* New Zealand: Reed Publishing (NZ) Ltd., 2000.

## LOOK IT UP!

**Maori Organizations of New Zealand**  www.maori.org/nz

**New Zealand on the Web**  www.nz.com/mainpage.html

# Glossary

**adorn** to add beauty or decorate something

**ancestor** a person, plant, animal, or object from a past generation

**Aotearoa** the traditional Maori name for New Zealand

**chisels** metal tools with a sharp edge that are used to cut or shape something

**cloaks** loose pieces of clothing that fasten around the neck

**cultures** groups of people who share customs, values, traditions, and beliefs

**dialect** a form of a language spoken in a different region

**fertility** producing something, especially a great deal of it

**flax** a fiber made from a commonly farmed plant that has pale blue flowers

**generation** people of the same age living in a society or family

**honed** made better

**indigenous peoples** the first settlers in a particular country or region

**looms** machines used to weave yarn or thread into cloth by weaving many strands together

**martial arts** fighting methods that use very specific movements

**missionaries** people who teach their religion to other cultures

**moa** a large ostrich-like bird that lived on Aotearoa; it could not fly and is now extinct

**prestige** a level of importance in the eyes of other people

**privileged** a person who has rights or benefits that not every person has

**rank** a position in society

**rite** a ceremonial act or action

**sacred** spiritual, religious, and holy

**sanitation** the use of special measures to ensure a clean environment; sewage disposal

**slaves** people who are forced to do physical work for other people

# Index

Aotearoa  4, 5, 7, 9, 18, 22, 24, 26, 27, 28

carving  10, 12, 18, 19, 20, 23, 24, 25, 26
cloak  21
clothes  18, 19, 20, 29
Cook, Captain James  9
Cooper, Dame Whina  27, 29

Elizabeth II  9, 28

food  5, 15, 21, 22, 23, 29, 30

Great Britain  9

haka  11, 16, 17, 19
hapu  8

marae  10, 14

New Zealand  4, 5, 8, 9, 11, 17, 26, 27, 28, 29, 30

Papatuanuku  6, 7
Polynesia  4, 22
Polynesian  5, 13, 18

rangatira  10
Ranginui  6, 7

stories  4, 5, 6, 7, 12, 16, 18

Tasman, Abel  8, 9
tohunga  10, 14, 20, 23

weapons  7, 8, 9, 11, 16, 17, 18, 19, 24, 25
whare  10

Young Maori Party  28

# Photograph Credits

Every reasonable effort has been made to trace ownership and to obtain permission to reprint copyright material. The publishers would be pleased to have any errors or omissions brought to their attention so that they may be corrected in subsequent printings.

**Cover:** Elizabeth Hanson / ADAMS / HANSEN PHOTOGRAPHY; **Archives New Zealand, Te Whare Tohu Tuhituhinga O Aotearoa Wellington Office:** page 29B [Alexander Turnbull Library, National Publicity Studios Collection ∏-040176 (NPS-A31014)]; **Corel Corporation:** pages 7T, 7B, 18B, 23; **CP/AAP (Marty Melville):** page 27; **James Heremaia:** pages 1, 3, 4T, 6T, 8T, 9, 10T, 10B, 11T, 11B, 12T, 12B, 13T, 13B, 14T, 14B, 15, 16, 17, 18T, 19T, 19B, 20T, 20B, 21T, 21B, 22T, 22M, 24T 25, 26T, 26B, 28T, 28B, 29T, 30; ©**WOLFGANG KAEHLER 2005 www.wkaehlerphoto.com:** pages 5, 6B, 24B; **Mary Evans Picture Library:** page 8B; **Photos.com:** page 22B.

**On the cover**
Maori children share and preserve their culture by participating in cultural activities.